19,000 **pounds of ice** used per day in the high season

RACHEL THE PIG weighs **700** lbs and raises an average of **$8,000** per year

10 million visitors per year

1,750 pounds of crab sold in a single day in the high season

6,500 rolls of toilet paper used every year in the north and south public restrooms

IIO people served per day at the senior

2,500 light fixtures in the common areas

50 organized school tours per year

5,000 tenants lock themselves out per year

3 major fires

500 people come to the Market's food bank—it is one of Seattle's busiest

35,000 visitors on a summer day

515 farmers rented tables in 1939

(up to) **200** buskers perform on a summer day

PIKE PLACE MARKET:

100 YEARS

THE PIKE PLACE MARKET
PRESERVATION & DEVELOPMENT
AUTHORITY

SASQUATCH BOOKS
SEATTLE

feeding Seattle's soul

Pike Place Market was born on August 17, 1907 as a city experiment to connect farmers directly with consumers. A century later, Pike Place Market is the nation's oldest continually operating farmers' market and is home to nearly 300 year-round commercial businesses; 190 craftspeople and 100 farmers who rent table space by the day; 240 street performers and musicians; and over 400 apartment units, most of which house low-income elderly people.

Seattle's icon, the Market attracts 10 million visitors each year from around the world. The Market's nine acres tell the story of our city and its people—stories of immigration, internment, gentrification, and urban renewal—that make it "The Soul of Seattle."

Throughout its first ten decades, the Market has had its ebbs and flows. In its youth, it grew into a vibrant, active marketplace where people gathered and shopped for their daily needs.

Mid-century, the Market entered a period of decline and a different aura took over, attracting a more eclectic type—the beatnicks and bohemians gathered at the

for 100 years. . .

Market and made it their own. The Market of today continues to be a favorite gathering place of people of all ages and backgrounds.

Two defining events in its 100 years had major impacts on the Market, one global and one local. World War II and the Japanese internment set off the Market's near demise. And the "Save the Market" initiative in the late 1960s rescued it from that demise. Both stories are shared in greater detail on the following pages.

The life of the Market as depicted through these pictures and descriptions represent what we in Seattle love about our Market. . . its people. After all, it's people who have "souls."

As you thumb through the pages, let yourself experience the past, savor the flavors, and get to know the people who make the Market.

summer

Summertime brings throngs of downtown workers, Seattle natives, and tourists to the cobblestone streets and hardwood interiors of the Market. In June, farmers show up with new crops of summer squash and fishmongers distribute fresh-caught salmon.

In the early 1900s, the rapid rise of produce prices—in one year, the price of onions multiplied ten-fold—led City Councilman Thomas Revelle to propose the creation of an official public market, where customers could buy produce directly from the producer. Eight farmers began selling on the rainy morning of August 17, 1907, the official opening day of the Pike Place Public Market, and were immediately overwhelmed by 10,000 customers. A tradition of "Meet the Producer" was born and continues to this day, in which the public meets and interacts with the makers, from the farmer who personally grows savory herbs or juicy cherries to the craftsperson who creates unique jewelry or forms exquisite pottery. The sounds of music also play a part in the Market's history: In the early days, vaudeville acts provided entertainment in the Market's Main Arcade. Nowadays, international entertainers of all genres perform throughout the Market. Today, the Market remains the "soul of Seattle," a meeting place for old friends and an icon of the Emerald City for new visitors.

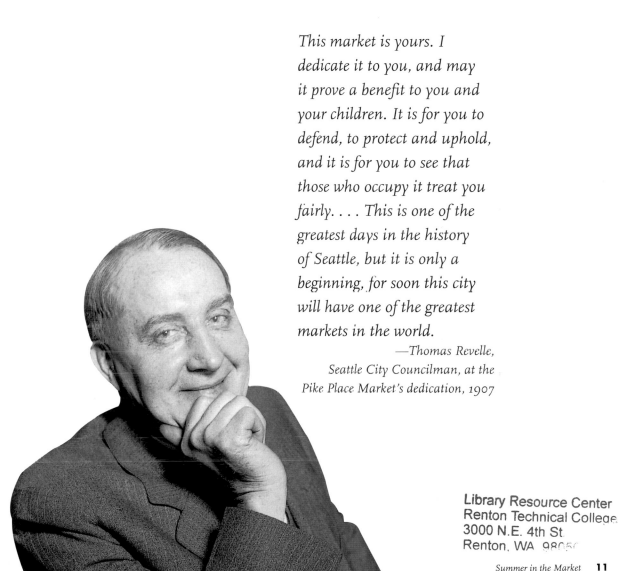

This market is yours. I dedicate it to you, and may it prove a benefit to you and your children. It is for you to defend, to protect and uphold, and it is for you to see that those who occupy it treat you fairly. . . . This is one of the greatest days in the history of Seattle, but it is only a beginning, for soon this city will have one of the greatest markets in the world.

—Thomas Revelle,
Seattle City Councilman, at the
Pike Place Market's dedication, 1907

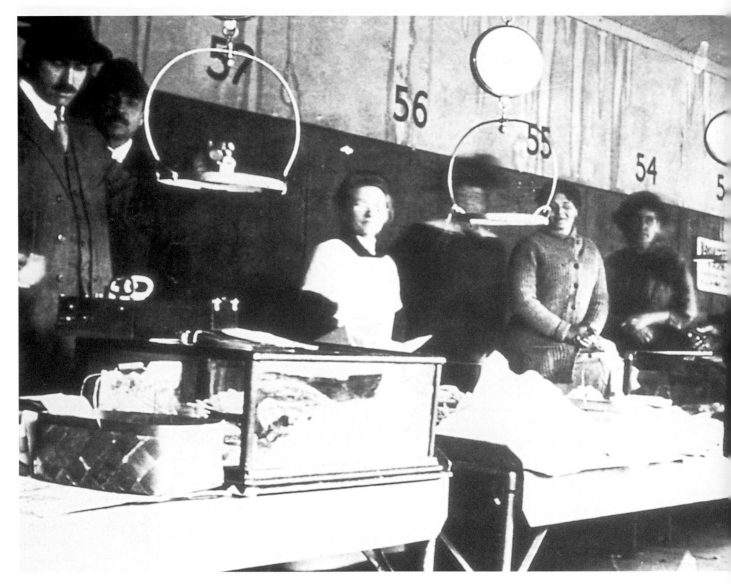

Customers were cautioned to check the scales lest merchants "let their hands linger lovingly on the cut, so that for every pound of meat they sell, a customer frequently pays for a quarter pound or more of hand." An agent from the Department of Weights and Measures inspects scales (left).

I remember one day when I tied up 225 dozen bunches of onions for the day. Sometimes we had to work until ten or eleven at night getting things ready, washing the carrots, tying the onions, loading up the truck. Then the next morning we would be up at 5 or 6 a.m. to pick some more before we left for town.

—Teresina Desimone,
A Lifetime in the Market,
Market News, 1977

Many Hmong and Mien people fled their homeland to escape death and persecution for assisting American soldiers during the Vietnam War. In 1982, the Market became a partner in the Indochinese Farm Project, an effort to help refugees become self-sufficient. Since then, more than thirty Hmong and Mien families have sold flowers and vegetables in the Market.

Asahel Curtis, brother of Edward Curtis, was
a prominent Seattle photographer during the
early twentieth century. He is best known for
his photographs of Washington State's natural
resources and their related industries. He took
many photos of the Market (including the photo
opposite, from 1931). He was also a founding
member of The Mountaineers, a renowned
outdoor recreation club.

To accompany the cacophony of telling, selling, and teasing, buskers and performers provide another, more deliberate soundtrack. If you like what you hear, tip them a buck or two and support the art in the air.

Music notes painted on sidewalks throughout the Market designate where the Market performers can play music, sing, or perform. Individuals or groups are allowed to perform at the same location for only one hour, after which they must move on to another spot.

Daystalls are the epitome of the "Meet the Producer" tradition in the Market. Products on the daystall tables are all made or grown by the person who rents the table. At left, Deanna Duff and her mother, Judy, gather greens at their family's farm.

A frugal, personable, and colorful figure, Giuseppe ("Joe") Desimone was a poor but ambitious Italian immigrant who began as a farmer in the Market in 1925. By 1941, he was president and owner of the Market. His legacy of loyalty to longtime Market tenants continues to guide Market policies under public ownership today.

The Market in the morning is a swell of activity. Deliveries arrive, ice flies, and boxes tumble. Farmers arrive at 6:30 in the morning to receive their table assignments, and by 9:00 A.M., craftspeople have lined up for their seniority-based roll call.

Highstalls are permanent produce stands that offer specialties from around the world, as well as regional produce. At the Market's Centennial in 2007, there were eight highstalls.

Jack Almeleh, right, and his brother Pinky were Sephardic Jews who came to Seattle in the 1920s and got jobs as fishmongers. Pinky's fear of knives prompted him to open a produce highstall, which he owned for over thirty years.

summer shopping list—

baby back ribs

ALBACORE TUNA

corn

peaches

strawberries

pears

sweet vidalia onions

BING, RAINIER, VAN, AND QUEEN ANNE CHERRIES

summer squash

blueberries

apricots *plums*

pea vines

limes

PICKLING CUCUMBERS

peppers: sweet banana, floral jim, firecracker, gold spike

TAYBERRIES

nectarines

gooseberries

FIGS: ADRIATIC,

BLACK MISSION,

BROWN TURKEY, KADOTA

red flame, thompson seedless grapes

Fresh salmon is a must in summer. The variety of salmon can determine how to best prepare it. Ask around the Market as you shop.

Tomatoes are a late-summer crop in Washington. Look for many varieties offered by Market farmers in September and October. At other times, shop the highstalls.

Stuff squash blossoms with chèvre cheese and sun-dried tomatoes, then lightly batter and fry to make memorable appetizers.

Hungry? The Market's many restaurants, cafés, take-out spots, and coffee shops can satisfy any craving. Choices range from fine Italian and French cuisine to Thai take-out to Northwest specialties. Linger over a glass of wine or dessert and coffee.

autumn

Harvest time in the Northwest—with sunny days and balmy breezes blowing through in September and October, this is a celebrated season. After the summertime swarm of tourists, locals return to browse the Market, seeking out their regular haunts and favorite vendors. Winter squash, peppers, and late-season corn fill the farm tables.

Autumn is also a time of celebration, for it was in November of 1971 that the Friends of the Market, led by Victor Steinbrueck, saved the Market from demolition. It is a story of rescue: that is, after urban decay spread through the Market in the 1950s and 1960s, the City of Seattle proposed redeveloping the Market into a plaza with a new hotel, four 28-story office buildings, and a hockey arena. Thanks to a grassroots public initiative, Seattle's voters responded overwhelmingly in favor of preserving the authentic use and culture of Pike Place Market. In particular, the Market was instructed to preserve its original focus on fresh produce and sustaining local farmers. And its mission lives on: Throughout the fall harvest, farmers sell Washington produce from easy-access tents along the cobblestone streets. And, as Washington State leads the nation in the production of apples, autumn is a particularly tasty time to experience the Market.

Commercial businesses in the Market are required to be small, owner-operated start-ups. Any large chain store you see here got its start at the Market. Starbucks's first cafe began serving their famous coffee in their Pike Place location in 1971. Just one year later, Sur La Table was established as a venue for culinary aficionados to purchase hard-to-find tools.

Three Girls Bakery began on the corner of First and Pike in 1912. Now housed on Pike Place, it remains one of Seattle's favorite sandwich-to-go spots.

The history of DeLaurenti's in the Market dates back to 1928 when Angelina Mustello opened a small store in the Market. Her daughter married Pete DeLaurenti, and they opened a second store in 1948. Their son, Louie, eventually took over, moving the shop up to its First Avenue location.

Four fish markets offer fresh fish and shellfish, and fishmongers can fillet, clean, and pack purchases for short or long trips home. Pure Food Fish Market was started in 1911 by Jack Amon. In 1956, his sons Sol and Irving purchased the business from their father. In 2006, Sol celebrated his fiftieth anniversary in the Market—and celebrated by giving his entire day's proceeds to the Market Foundation.

Filipino immigrants began arriving in Seattle in the 1920s. They worked on farms and later bought land from the Japanese who were interned in 1942. Among the famous Filipino farm families of the 1950s through the 1980s were Casey and Lucille Cruz, Primo and Frances Primero, Alex Molina, Tom Viloria, and Rufinio and Tina Ordonio (pictured above).

Many ethnic food stores and specialty grocers are located in the Market. Fiery peppers, unusual grains, exotic fruits, and much more await today's Market shopper. Ask questions when you see unusual items— you'll learn about other foods and other cultures.

Italian families have been selling in the Market from the start. In the early twentieth century, there were so many Italian farmers in the Rainier Valley that it became known as "Garlic Gulch." With names like Ditore, Vacca, Genzale, Manzo, Ferrucci, Pelligrini, Desimone, LoPriore, Ianniciello, and Fuffaro, these vendors became Market fixtures and so did their descendents.

In 1947, Morris Levy, pictured at right, challenged a new City Council policy that forbade singing vendors. Sue Manzo shushed him in the background. Members of the Manzo family still own two highstalls.

SPECIAL
UTAH TYPE CELERY
20 ¢ EA

SOLID HEAD LETTUCE
2 FOR..15

autumn shopping list—

valencia oranges

BRATWURST

peppers

FUYU AND pistachios

HACHIYA PERSIMMONS

daikon tomatoes

steak

delicious, gala

golden

winesap,

red delicious,

apples:

SHUNGIKU quince pumpkins

grapes

dill

WALLA WALLA ONIONS

red leaf
green leaf
lettuce

mustard

greens *basil*

TURKEY

pomegranate

cardoon **meat** **stew** *yams*

APPLES: FUJI, ROME, GRANNY SMITH, CRITERION, TSUGARU, SPARTAN, KING

cranberries, huckleberries

Early autumn in the Market requires firm
decision-making skills and a set of strong arms—
produce bags are heavy! The variety of farm-fresh
produce is endless. Though the growing season
comes to a close, autumn provides parting gifts
of fresh potatoes, tomatoes, onions, green beans,
and raw honey.

Old-fashioned meat markets will slice your steak to the thickness you desire and offer many special cuts.

When shopping for produce and fish, ask what's in season— seasonal items are typically fresher and sometimes cheaper. Gather cooking tips and inquire about different ways to prepare and enjoy what you buy. All of the fresh items on the farm tables are locally grown crops. Some farmers offer preserved items (like herb-flavored vinegars and berry jams) that they have made with their own crops.

More than half of all apples grown in the United States for fresh eating come from orchards in Washington State. Market farmers offer a variety of apples; ask which are best for eating, baking, drying, or making applesauce. Harvest time is September and October, but local apples remain available much of the year.

By the 1950s, the once indispensable Market had become neglected and decayed. The post–World War II move to suburban areas and the subsequent popularity of grocery stores and frozen foods had all but deadened the need for public markets. Concerned about the image and future of Seattle, a group of businessmen formed the Central Business Association, looking to federal urban renewal grants to raze the dilapidated Pike Place Market and revitalize Downtown with high-rise apartments, hotels, and office buildings.

[The Market] reveals the face of truth.
Its roughness reminds me of Seattle's
beginning, its lusty past, the vitality
that gave it national notice long ago.
It is an honest place in a phony time.
                                    —*Fred Bassetti*

ERLING
ENTRANCE

In 1964, Victor Steinbrueck, a self-taught architect and professor at the University of Washington, formed Friends of the Market, a group dedicated to saving and renewing the historic Public Market—its structures, farmers, small businesses, and low-income residents. Steinbrueck led the Friends in obtaining twenty thousand signatures to force a city-wide public vote to "Keep the Market."

VOTE YES

PIKE PLACE MARKET INITIATIVE

LET'S KEEP THE MARKET

CITY ELECTION NOV. 2

FRIENDS OF THE MARKET
Victor Steinbrueck, Pres.

LAST CHANCE TO SAVE THE

PIKE PLACE MARKET

SEATTLE CITY COUNCIL

PUBLIC HEARING

APRIL 18-FRIDAY MORNING 9:00 AM till NOON
SEATTLE MUNICIPAL BUILDING-11 th FLOOR

CITIZENS OF SEATTLE & KING COUNTY: In the name of common decency, and the tradition and heritage of our region, the FRIENDS OF THE MARKET summon you to our cause of keeping this low-cost market now existing in the Pike Place Market area for all people for now and for the future.

Having worked for many years for the continuity and improvement of the market and having given voice to the concern of more than 52,000 people through a supporting petition and many other efforts, having patiently waited for sympathetic understanding and response from our City Council all to little apparent avail—we must now call for aggressive action from concerned people lest the cause be lost.

Only an aroused citizenry can keep them from making the decision to wreck the people's market and Seattle's prime attraction for the sake of a grandiose private land grab subsidized to more than $18,000,000 by the taxpayers from the federal and city pocketbooks.

The central business MERCHANTS OF GREED are using URBAN RENEWAL to MURDER THE MARKET: by strangulation and rape thru demolition and disruption of the entire area for more than four years, by taking the heart of the market to give life to their swank hotel and luxury apartment plaza development, by costly changes in that remaining market core to make it palatable to their plush plastic plaza as a phony and nostalgic vestige of the past, by relocating and driving out most of the businesses and farmers thru rent raises and demolition, by eliminating First Avenue north of Union Street for five blocks to Lenora Street as a people's street, by relocating all of the 600 people now living there, and in all ways consciously destroying the low-cost shopping which is sorely needed by thousands of people while devesting the public that the market is being "saved".

No one can honestly believe that the people's market can survive such an onslaught of the federal bulldozer directed and driven by selfish self-serving "crass interests".

The existing people's public market must be kept because:
- It is the only LOW COST SHOPPING area on the West Coast. It is needed and it is irreplaceable.
- It is the only place in the region where people of every color, creed, economic status, and age group are welcome to shop, work, and browse in harmony and equality. There are no integration problems in the market.
- It is Seattle's only real and unique tourist attraction.
- It is the thriving symbol of the American ideal of small merchants, farmers, and individuals successfully and independently operating.

The FRIENDS OF THE MARKET demand that the city develop an alternate plan which: respects the people needing the market, using it, working there, and living there; gives these people a real voice in the planning; produces immediate improvement through sympathetic rehabilitation of buildings rather than demolition; assures retention of present businesses and farmers through maintenance of present businesses and farmers through maintenance of present rentals; provides for present residents to continue living there fittingly; and treats the entire Pike Place area as a neighborhood. However it must contribute to the life of the low-cost market and its people.

We encourage provision for additional and rehabilitated housing for all income brackets downtown.

WRITE TO ALL CITY COUNCIL MEMBERS telling them that they cannot do this to your market and that you support the position of the Friends of the Market. The Council members are: Paul J. Alexander, Ted Best, Charles M. Carroll, Mrs. Harlan H. Edwards, Tim Hill, Mrs. Arthur V. Langlonce, M. B. Mitchell, and Sam Smith. Their address is Seattle Municipal Building, 98104.

COME TO THE PIKE PLAZA HEARING and get others to come. Support the market and speak your mind out. Let us be resolved to keep this market that each generation may discover it anew.

(Signed)
FRIENDS OF THE MARKET, 91 PIKE PLACE, 98101—Ma. 2-2595

PUBLIC
MARKET
CENTER

FARMERS MARKET

MARKET THEATER
A FILM BY JONATHAN DEMME AND
TALKING HEADS
STOP MAKING SENSE
DAILY 5 45 8 10 15

In 1971, the initiative to save the Market and designate the area as a Historical District passed. In 1973, the Pike Place Market Preservation and Development Authority (PDA) was chartered by the City of Seattle to manage most of the properties in the nine-acre Market Historical District.

The PDA has charter responsibilities to preserve, rehabilitate, and protect the Market's buildings; increase opportunities for farm and food retailing in the Market; incubate and support small and marginal businesses; and provide services for low-income people.

winter

Locals and visitors alike find a more relaxed Market
in the wintertime. It's the perfect season to meander
through the DownUnder, a cozy warren of collectible
and antique shops located beneath the Market's Main
Arcade; to stop and chat with the shopkeepers and
learn the history of their store; or to linger over a
hot meal and comforting conversation in one of the
Market's many restaurants.

The chilly, dark winter days are also a time to remember and reflect upon a bleak point in the Market's history. On February 19, 1942, two months after the bombing of Pearl Harbor, President Franklin D. Roosevelt signed Executive Order 9066, which ultimately led to the nationwide incarceration of 110,000 Americans of Japanese ancestry. Most Japanese American farmers were forced to sell their businesses and property with only one month's notice. The order devastated the Market, as well as the lives of Japanese Americans. The number of farmer-seller licenses in the Market dropped by nearly 80 percent. The internment of the Japanese Americans was the start of a decline of the Pike Place Market—one that lasted until the early 1970s when, thanks to the citizens of Seattle, the Market was saved and reborn as a Historic District. As is characteristic of the Pike Place Market and members of its community, it perseveres. Now on winter nights, the lights of the Market's grand Arcade shine brighter than ever—a symbol of our treasured Market's enduring spirit.

Check out the DownUnder for unique retail experiences.

Holidays are a time for giving, and Rachel—
the Market Foundation's piggy bank—is happy
to do her part to bring home the bacon. From
her spot under the Market clock, she raises
$6,000–9,000 each year for the Market's four
human service agencies—its Medical Clinic,
Senior Center, Child Care and Preschool, and
Food Bank. Together, they provide groceries,
hot meals, child care, health care, employment
and housing services, and counseling for
more than ten thousand low-income seniors,
families, and downtown workers each year.

The Market is home to more than four
hundred people who live in the apartments
above the shops. Most are low-income seniors.

The "Pave the Market Arcade" tile project began in 1985 as a way to restore the Main Arcade's rotting wooden floor. Local businesses and individuals made donations to the Market in exchange for an imprinted tile. In all, 46,500 tiles were laid.

Artists of all mediums and walks of life are
drawn to the Market's constant activity. Artist
Mark Tobey's book of paintings (including
E Pluribus Unum, left), as well as lithographs
he donated to Friends of the Market, played
an integral part in raising funds for the ballot
initiative that made the Market a Historic
District. Victor Steinbrueck, credited for his
leadership in the battle that saved the Market
from an urban renewal plan that would have
demolished it, spent a decade sketching the
nuances and spirit of the Market (right).

R.C. (right) is the mastermind behind Post Alley's famous poster wall.

HEART
OF
THE
PUBLIC
MARKET.

SARAH JANE LAPP 4.03

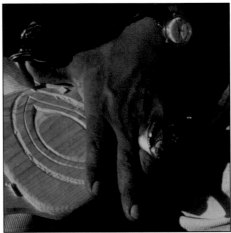

Find a unique gift or memento of your trip
to the Pike Place Market on the North Arcade
daystalls, where local craftspeople sell a
fascinating array of their own handmade
creations throughout the year.

winter shopping list—

prime rib roast

geese

KING SALMON

mussels

fresh duck

crab

clams

crown roast pork or lamb

TENDERLOINS: CHÂTEAUBRIAND, BEEF WELLINGTON

broccoli

BRUSSELS

chard

d'anjou

pears *dates*

EGGPLANT

wild mushrooms

potatoes:
red, white,
gold, Yukon,
purple

SPROUTS

grapefruit

kale okra

turnips

WINTER SQUASH:

ACORN, DELICATA,

SPAGHETTI, PUMPKIN

mandarins, tangerines, lemons

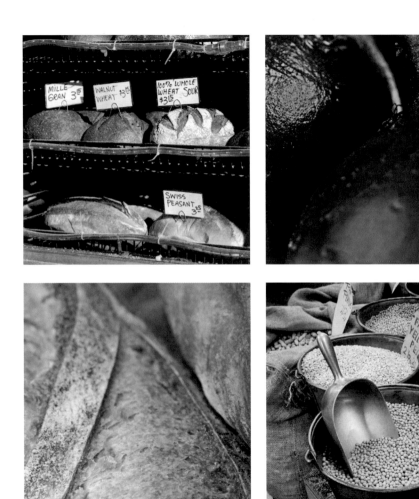

The holiday season brings an abundance of specialty meats, cheeses, and ingredients. Place orders for specialty items or those that might be in high demand.

Winter is a great time to explore the Market for culinary ingredients, whether you're making a gourmet feast or a favorite comfort food. Stews and soups are especially popular when the weather turns chilly, so stock up on root vegetables and grains, and don't forget a crusty loaf of bread.

Penn Cove mussels from Whidbey Island are suspended below rafts and never experience low tide; this means they can feed nonstop and are cultivated to be as plump as possible. Depending on their size, oysters can be eaten raw or cooked. The diminutive Kumomoto oysters are sweet when eaten raw. Hood Canal oysters are best poached, fried, or grilled. Quilcenes, ever versatile, can be enjoyed either way.

Since day one, various immigrant communities have formed the backbone of the Market's success. With each wave of world history, the Market becomes home to new cultures. Most prominent have been the Italians, Japanese, Filipinos, Sephardic Jews, and Southeast Asians.

In April 1942, as World War II began, all people of Japanese ancestry were ordered to leave Seattle—an estimated population of seven thousand. Since many of those families were farmers and vendors, the impact on the Market was devastating.

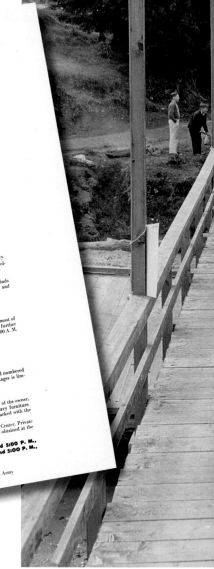

Japanese American farmers on Bainbridge Island were Market producers and sellers. In 1942, they were evacuated from the island by Executive Order 9066.

A mural at the entrance to the Main Arcade commemorates the effects of internment on the Market. In 1939, there were 515 Japanese American farmers selling at the Market. In 1949, there were 53.

spring

In a burst of golden yellow, spring kicks off
with Daffodil Day, a Market tradition of passing
out blooms to passers-by along the streets of Seattle.
Heralding the advent of sunny skies, spring crops,
and longer days, this golden flower is a fitting gift,
given that the Market was largely built from spoils
of the Klondike Gold Rush.

And Seattle boasts a golden past: In the early 1900s, this city was the gateway to the Klondike River as thousands of prospectors headed north in pursuit of wealth. Frank Goodwin was one of a handful who survived the arduous Alaskan conditions and made his fortune, settling in Seattle with $50,000 worth of gold dust and nuggets. Goodwin invested his gold in Pike Place Market property, purchasing numerous buildings, including the Leland Hotel, and designing the first farmer stalls along the Pike Place sidewalks. By 1911, what would eventually become the North Arcade had expanded from Pike Place to Stewart Street, offering fresh wares from farmers, fishmongers, and butchers. Each spring, farmers sell fresh peas, onions, and broccoli.

The Pike Place Market Street Festival began as
a thank-you to the citizens of Seattle for their
vote to save the Market from demolition in 1971.
Now, the annual festival is not only a thank-
you to Seattle's citizens but also a grand display
of handcrafted work, culinary delights, and a
showcase of colorful local music.

Though it is public, Pike Place Market does not receive any public money for its ownership and operation.

During the summer of 2001, 170 whimsically decorated life-size pigs—each in the image of the Market's beloved piggy bank, Rachel—hogged Seattle sidewalks. Some of the un–decorated offspring remain on rooftops and appear as "swinedeer" during the holidays. Pigs on Parade, repeated with 100 pigs in 2007, celebrated both the Chinese Year of the Pig and the Market's Centennial.

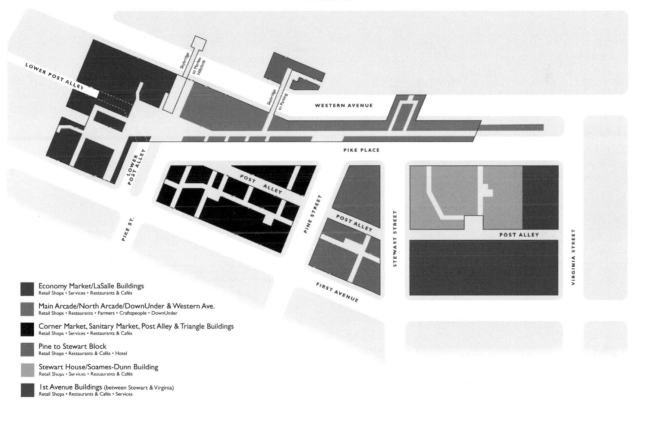

MARKET OVERVIEW MAP

NORTH ▶

ELLIOTT BAY

ALASKAN WAY

LOWER POST ALLEY

Skybridge to Market HallsInfo

Skybridge to Parking

WESTERN AVENUE

LOWER POST ALLEY

PIKE PLACE

POST ALLEY

POST ALLEY

POST ALLEY

PINE STREET

PIKE ST.

STEWART STREET

VIRGINIA STREET

FIRST AVENUE

Economy Market/LaSalle Buildings
Retail Shops • Services • Restaurants & Cafés

Main Arcade/North Arcade/DownUnder & Western Ave.
Retail Shops • Restaurants • Farmers • Craftspeople • DownUnder

Corner Market, Sanitary Market, Post Alley & Triangle Buildings
Retail Shops • Services • Restaurants & Cafés

Pine to Stewart Block
Retail Shops • Restaurants & Cafés • Hotel

Stewart House/Soames-Dunn Building
Retail Shops • Services • Restaurants & Cafés

1st Avenue Buildings (between Stewart & Virginia)
Retail Shops • Restaurants & Cafés • Services

In 1927, the legendary red neon clock was constructed above the Main Arcade, serving as the icon for the flourishing Pike Place Market.

In 1910, the Sanitary Public Market opened across Pike Place from the Main Market. It justified its name by barring horses from its interior. The adjacent Corner Market Building opened in 1912. Two years later, Goodwin erected the vertical maze of the Fairley Building (Main Market), which today houses mostly retail shops.

By the time this photo was taken in 1948, the neon clock had become the Market's icon. Built in 1900, the Bartell Drugs Building at First and Pike was originally the stable for farmers' horses. It was renamed the Economy Market Building because it was the discount and day-old section of the Market.

After World War II, the Outlook Hotel was renamed the LaSalle Hotel by owner Nellie Curtis, an entrepreneurial businesswoman who bought it from the Kodama family during the 1942 evacuation and turned the building into a popular brothel. In 1951, Curtis sold the hotel to another Japanese American family, the Ikedas, who restored its original use as a hotel. The LaSalle was renovated in the 1970s to become forty low-income senior apartments and re-renovated in 2006, increasing the amount of housing for low-income seniors to sixty-four and adding a new home for the Market's Senior Center.

spring shopping list—

corned beef

carrots

COPPER RIVER SALMON

collards
fennel
rhubarb

bone-in ham

garlic

artichoke

fava beans

MUSHROOMS:
PORTABELLO, BELLY-BUTTON
HEDGEHOG

fiddlehead

cabbage

ferns *lamb*

morels

BABY BOK CHOY

HALIBUT

cauliflower

spring salad mix

asparagus

green onions

kumquats

MINEOLA TANGELOS

HONEY TANGERINES

BLOOD & NAVEL ORANGES

sweet pink grapefruit

Pasquelina Verdi started selling her produce in 1955 and earned the title "Queen of the Market." One of her special sales techniques was to place a mystery item in her customers' bags to ensure they'd return to ask for preparation advice.

FRESH
RHUBARB
5¢
lb
3 lbs
10¢

NEW
RADISH
4
BUNCHES
5¢

SWEET
ONIONS
4
BUNCHES
5¢

Today, the ever-growing population of urban residents in the downtown area flock to the Market for fresh produce, artisanal cheeses, and seasonal seafood. A world-renowned tourist attraction, the Market is once again utilized as it was originally intended—a gathering place for producers to sell directly to the public.

art credits and permissions

acknowledgments

For 100 years, the Pike Place Market has exemplified the meaning of community in Seattle. And, true to the spirit of the Market, countless people worked to help piece together this chronicle of its first century. Some contributors hail from within the nine acres the Market occupies and some from the outside—but all share a common love of this place.

This book sits before you because of the work of the staff, supporters, and friends of the Pike Place Market and the Market Foundation: Pike Place Market community members; Sasquatch Books; 100 Cameras; Horton Lantz & Low; all featured photographers and artists; all sources who granted use of photography, art, and reproductions of any kind; and all contributing writers and editors.

Any omission of due credit is the responsibility and oversight of the Pike Place Market Preservation and Development Authority.

Printed in Singapore
  by Star Standard Industries Pte Ltd.
Published by Sasquatch Books
Distributed by Publishers Group West
15 14 13 12 11 10 09 08 07 06   9 8 7 6 5 4 3 2 1

Front cover photograph: John Wiley
Back cover photograph: *The Seattle Times*
Rain in Seattle (painting): © Greta Wilson
Cover design, interior design, and composition: Finally Dunn Productions

Library of Congress Cataloging-in-Publication Data is available.

ISBN 1-57061-497-0

Sasquatch Books
119 South Main Street, Suite 400
Seattle, WA 98104
(206) 467-4300
www.sasquatchbooks.com
custserv@sasquatchbooks.com

19,000 pounds of ice used per day in the high season

10 million visitors per year

1,750 pounds of crab sold in a single day in the high season

6,500 rolls of toilet paper used every year in the north and south public restrooms

RACHEL THE PIG weighs **700** lbs and raises an average of **$8,000** per year

110 people served per day at the senior

2,500 light fixtures in the common areas

50 organized school tours per year

5,000 tenants lock themselves out per year

3 major fires

35,000 visitors on a summer day

500 people come to the Market's food bank—it is one of Seattle's busiest

515 farmers rented tables in 1939

(up to) **200** buskers perform on a summer day